MTV
MUSIC TELEVISION®

BOOK NO.

02

OVERGROUND

First published in the United States of
America in 2003
by UNIVERSE PUBLISHING
A Division of Rizzoli International
Publications, Inc.
300 Park Avenue South
New York, NY 10010
www.rizzoliusa.com

2003 2004 2005 2006 2007 / 10 9 8 7 6 5
4 3 2 1

Printed in China

Library of Congress Catalog Control
Number: 2003104733

BOARDS

The Art + Design of the Skateboard

Edited by Jacob Hoye

Designed by Rockpants

Art Editor: Walter Einenkel

Universe

For Lucas

INTRO:

INSPIRATION: I took a Polaroid once of the wall of boards at Supreme, one of the preeminent skate shops (Lafayette Street, NYC). I wanted to capture the colors and the vibrant ideas. The wall there appears more like an art installation than a display of commercial goods or products. Available light seemed sufficient enough. I fit the wall in the square of the viewfinder. A click. The shutter held a second longer than I expected. My hand shook. The developing image blurred as if the energy from the boards trembled too hard to be contained in the frame of a photograph.

INFLUENCE: Skateboarding has always had a deep connection to subversion. The sport, to speak in general terms, is inherently individualistic, willful, arrogant, dangerous. Think of terms like "skate rat" or "skate punk" or the ongoing battle between authority and skaters over control of the public space. In New York, street stylists refuse to be confined to designated skate parks or vert-o-ramas. They want to grind benches, wallride facades, tailslide monument bases. In short, they want to cover the same terrain as pedestrians, and then some. Essentially, when it comes to skating, it's about the experience of liberation: getting higher, moving faster, grinding longer, sliding smoother, etc.

INTENTION: Despite the mainstreaming of skateboarding in recent years, it still carries with it an implied sense of menace, the vague aura of a counterculture. It's fitting then that deck design embodies those same traits. The art and design of the skateboard is as diverse as the pros and amateurs that ride them. Inside these pages, you'll see an amalgamation of counterculture and popular culture. Deck designers appropriate any and everything for their own purposes, churning out a sick mix of radical graphics, refined illustrations, obnoxious art and beautiful imagery. Viewed collectively, it's clear that some of the most exciting work in the design world is happening right under your feet. Deck designers, like skaters, just don't seem to give a fuck about what people think. And why should they when their work is just going to wind up a smudge on some block of cement?

Jacob Hoye, Editor

Skateboards are almost like posters, or t-shirts,

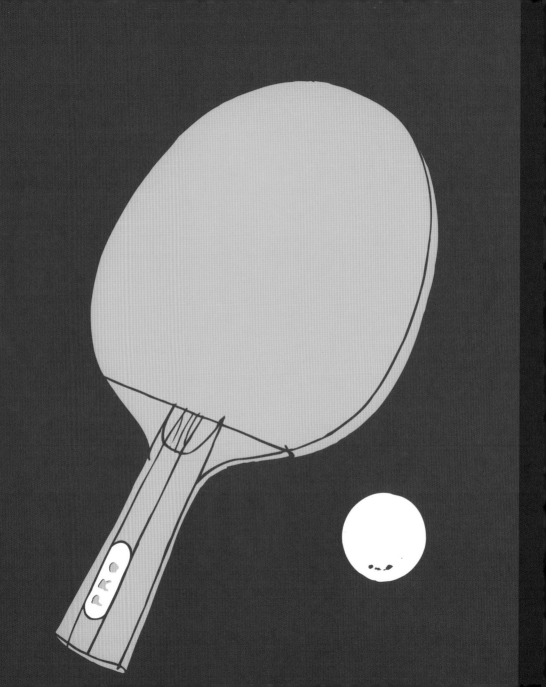

there is a lot of potential for the designs to communicate.

I feel like most of my board designs are just

intended to be cool-looking images,

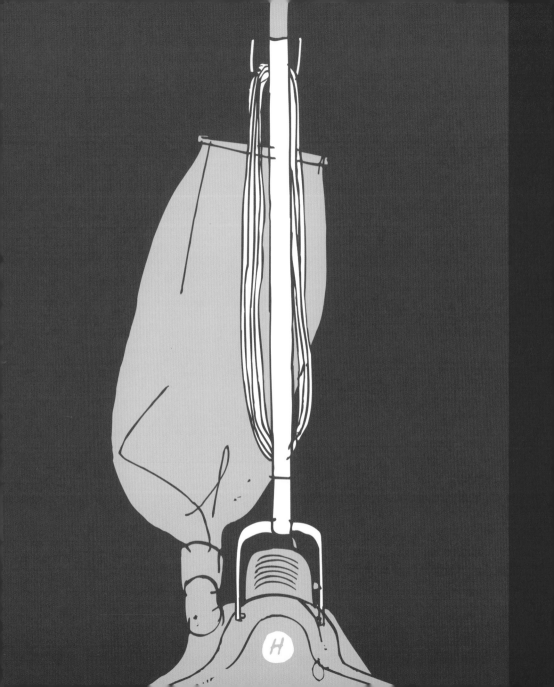

but I think I would like to move more toward idea-based designs

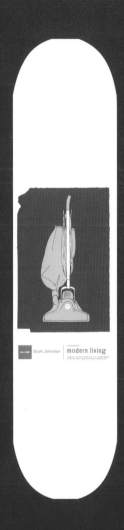

that communicate concepts and inspire thought.

—evan hecox

5boro   *Bridge*   Artist: Mark Nardelli

5boro *On time* Artist: Trollback & co.

5boro *Post* Artist: Rob Mars

5boro   *Garage*   Artist: Rob Mars

5boro   *Subway*   Artist: Mark Nardelli

MARK NARDELLI
ARTIST, 5BORO SKATEBOARDS

Influences are rooted in things that are not related to what I am designing. I could be designing a skateboard graphic and find ideas in a furniture catalog. With 5boro it is usually a much looser structure thematically and you can just make things that look good on the bottom of a skateboard. Rolling in New York is always an influence.

My scrapbook is where I keep my creative flow, but design is inspired by personal trends with myself. Like small wheels, big pants, then big wheels, small pants. I'm usually into collage stuff, but lately its been more clean shapes. Next batch of boards I want to do in a more hand drawn-style.

For 5boro, I want to just derive more elements from the city from Con Ed manhole covers to the people on the streets and ride them with the 5.

5boro   *Suski Eyes*   Artist: Ross Imms

Betty Boards
Artist: Sean Tubridy

BETTYBOARDS

enjoi

Most companies sort of do their own thing. I think there is too much importance
placed on series graphics, though. I think of people as individuals, and sometimes a
design that is particular to their character is in order. Series graphics are amazing,
too, if done well. I guess it's all relative. Everyone does what they want. I think the
emphasis put on board design is a really good thing. Design alone says the most about
your particular company.
—Marc Johnson, Artist

enjoi
appliance **series**
artist: judson bryan

enjoi

ltd. edition
artist: marc johnson
pro: marc johnson

hepburn
artist: marc johnson
pro: louie barletta

london calling
artist: marc johnson
pro: louie barletta

want shit
artist: marc johnson
pro: marc johnson

handstand helmet
artist: marc johnson
pro: dave mayhew

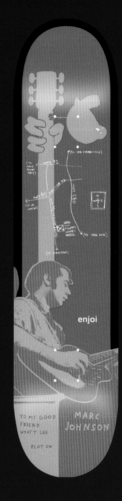

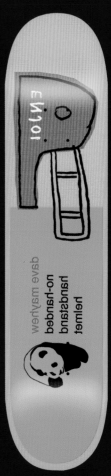

marc johnson
artist, enjoi

Influences:
Mostly I'm influenced by the "progressive" design work from the 50s and 60s. Designers like Paul Rand and Saul Bass and Hans Schleger. During that time those guys were concentrating on boldness and simplicity in design, which, then, was considered new and progressive. I'm influenced by all kinds of things. Who knows where it comes from? The skateboarders on enjoi influence the subject matter for many of the graphics, as a lot of what we do at enjoi is based around the personalities of the team.

Inspiration:
The inspiration for the work varies. It's usually something about a particular skateboarder, and the idea is hopefully broken down into an image that may or may not translate well into a board graphic. Sometimes the inspiration comes from art deadlines.

Intention:
We split the intention of the work between two things: First and foremost, we want the riders happy (if it's possible) with their graphic, as it is a representation of them. Secondly, we want the graphics to stand out on a skate-shop wall. We try as best we can to use color and composition to attract attention to the board, and then the subject matter of the graphic will hopefully make the buyer laugh or think. Some of the graphics are nonsensical, and others can be somber and subtle. We hope each kind will say something to the viewer about what we are trying to do with enjoi.

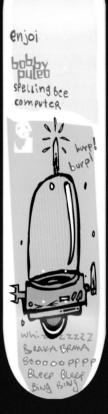

enjoi

broke junk series
artist: judson bryan
pro: louie barletta

broke junk series
artist: judson bryan
pro: dave mayhew

broke junk series
artist: judson bryan
pro: bobby puleo

broke junk series
artist: judson bryan
pro: brad staba

dingleberries 2
artist: judson bryan

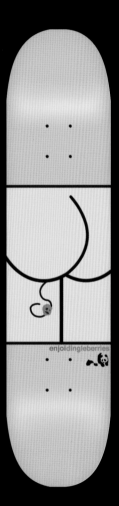

ZOO YORK

BALSA SERIES
Artist: Eli M. Gesner

NYC

ZooYork DECKS

100% • HAND • MADE

From the woods of Upstate New York comes
Todd Jordan. Zoo York was his first sponsor and
he's been with us ever since. Now, we're proud
to introduce Todd Jordan's first Pro Model.
Congratulations!

100% EAST COAST
SINCE 1993

One Wood Deck
Un Planche De Bois No. 05

TODD JORDAN

NYC

ZooYork DECKS

100% • HAND • MADE

Raised in the rough and tumble streets
of the Bronx, New York, Danny Supa
'popped' on to the international street skating
scene in the mid 90's thanks to his
incredible 'switch-stance' skills.

100% EAST COAST
SINCE 1993

One Wood Deck
Un Planche De Bois No. 01

DANNY SUPA

Marketing Series

Zoo York
Artist: Eli M. Gesner

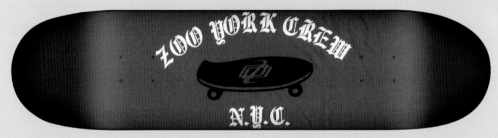

Zoo York   Artist: Eli M. Gesner

ZOO YORK

PRACTICE TRUTH · FEAR NOTHING

ZOO YORK

ZOO YORK

THE ZOO YORK INSTITUTE: REGISTERED FIELD OPERATIVE / 212718917646....

THIS UNIT IS A DIVISION 'A' TROOP TRANSPORT AND IS INTENDED FOR USE BY REGISTERED OPERATIVES ONLY . THIS UNIT ACTS AS THE PRIMARY COUPLING HUB FOR SPECIALIZED VEHICLE DEVICES. W440. W462 (URETHANE, BEARING HOUSABLE WHEELS AND SPECIALIZED VEHICLE DEVICES: T211S . T214S (ALLOY FORGED AXLE HANGER) AS WELL AS THE SUB COMPONENTS: 18E.2 . 18E7 (SHIELDED AXLE BEARING) . GT07 (ADHESIVE BACKED TRACTION TAPE), MH7S . MH42S (LOCK NUT MOUNTING BOLT) AND OTHER SPECIALIZED ACCESSORIES . MANY DIFFERENT VARIABLES ARE POSSIBLE WHEN ASSEMBLING. REGISTERED FIELD AGENTS SHOULD REFER TO HANDBOOK FOR ITEM LISTS AND SPECIFICATIONS . IMPROPER ASSEMBLY OF THIS TRANSPORT MAY RESULT IN INJURY TO THE FIELD AGENT . BE SURE THAT ONLY EXPERIENCED FIELD AGENTS OR TRANSPORT SPECIALISTS CONFIGURE THIS TRANSPORT FOR USAGE.

ZOO YORK

NEW YORKS FINEST . ALL CITY KINGS . FIVE BORO BRED THOROUGHBRED . NON PERPETRATIONAL . THE ACTUAL ARTICLE . PRACTICE TRUTH . FEAR NOTHING

212.718.917.646 · 1976.2001.NYC.USA

Zoo York   *Jest* Series   Artist: Eli M. Gesner

ZOO YORK
TODD JORDAN
· versus jest ·

ZOO YORK
DANNY SUPA
· versus jest ·

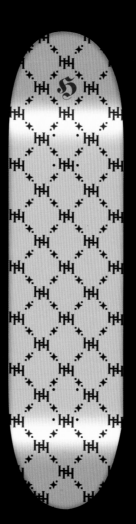

ZOO YORK
PRO: HAROLD HUNTER
ARTIST: ELI M. GESNER

communication series

...ue wo muite arukoh...
...anatano soba niha itumo
...a.....kokoro. kokoro ....
.... kitto okunohoh....

rookie skateboards

artist: Beci Orpin

rookie skateboards

artist: Elska Sandor

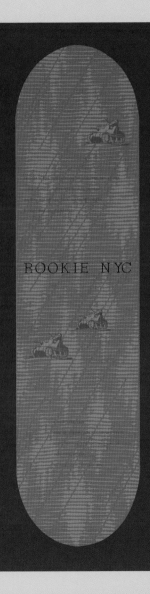

ROOKIE NYC

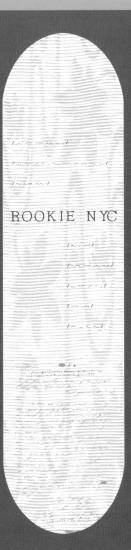

Girl Skateboards
Template OG Series
Artist: Andy Mueller
Pro: Mike Carrol

Girl Skateboards
Template OG **Series**
Artist: Andy Mueller
Pro: Mike Ferguson

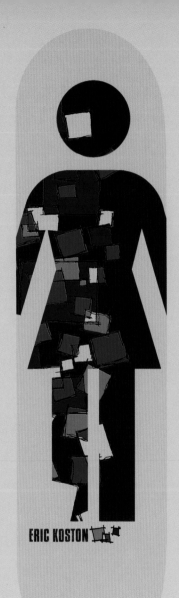

Girl Skateboards
Template OG Series
Artist: Tony Larson
Pro: Eric Koston

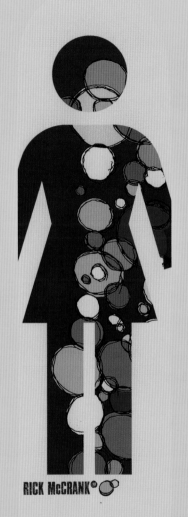

RICK McCRANK

Girl Skateboards
Template OG **Series**
Artist: Tony Larson
Pro: Rick McCrank

Girl

Template OG Series
artist: rob abeyta jr.

Rob Abeyta Jr.
Artist, Girl

Influences:
I'm not too into graphic design, really. But I do like NEASDEN CC, Artdump, Buffmonster, KR, Cy Twombly, peeling-wheatpasted-broken cement walls, old CTA buses, gang logos, tattoos, Cassavetes, Oriol, and people that have lived "the life."

Inspiration:
Sesame Street, Funny Garbarge, GIANTONE

Intention:
Marketability. Simplicity. Something new. A darn good "eye-grabber."

aesthetics

We wanted to have a series of skateboards with authentic-looking graphics for each rider, using our favorite games from the early 80s.

—Alex Aronovich, Artist

GAME SERIES

sal barbier 7 3/4 x 31 3/4

clyde singleton 7 9/16 x 31 3/8

kevin taylor 7 1/2 x 31 3/16

rob welsh 7 9/16 x 31 1/4

kevin taylo

7 1/2 x 31 3/16

aesthetics

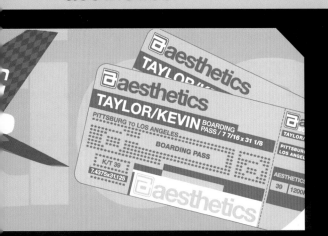

We simply wanted to have bold illustrations of cool, nonmilitary airplanes. The airline tickets on the tail of the deck had everything from the rider's name, to the dimensions of the deck. The tickets also featured each rider's hometown in the form of their departure point. All of the rider's tickets were arriving in Los Angeles, where the Aesthetics offices are located.

— Alex Aronovich, Artist

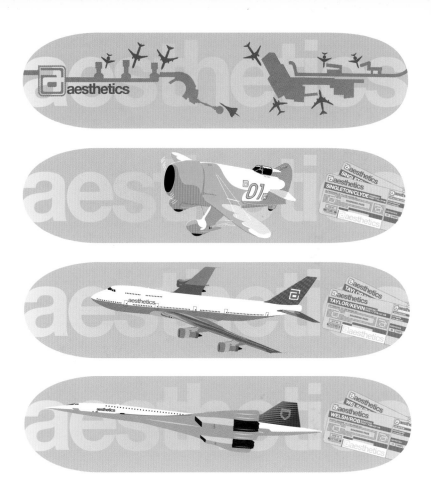

aesthetics
aviation series
artist: alex aronovich

It's the whole long and skinny thing that really gets my goat. Don't get me wrong, skateboards should not be short and fat, it's just that I believe the damn popsicle canvas may have ultimately crippled my professional life. Heck, the very idea of having to draw anything conforming to a square scares the absolute crap out of me. Luckily, the dimensions of a skateboard don't appear to be changing drastically anytime soon, so I've got a few good years left before obsolescence boots me into the artistic halfway house.
- Sean Cliver, Artist

Sean Cliver
Artist, Hook-Ups

Influences:
Let's just say I'm about as culturally deficient in the art history category as a kid bangin' in Little Rock, Arkansas. I've got a remedial grasp of the subject with most of my inspirations coming from pop culture crap like animation, comics and skateboards. Early on I really liked the artwork done by Dave Sims, Bob Burden, Robert Crumb, Dave McKean, and Steve Rude. Now I get happy when I see new stuff by the likes of Andy Jenkins, Joe Sorren, Thomas Campbell, Jeff Tremaine, Marc McKee, Ed Templeton, Chris Pontius, and a few odd others I cannot recall at the moment. I'd be just about the biggest idiot in the world if I didn't say V. Courtland Johnson had the greatest impact on my illustrative skills, though. VCJ used to be the old Powell Peralta artist back in the late 70s and most of the 80s up until he quit and I soiled the graphic history at the company in 1989.

Inspiration:
Obviously it's heavily influenced by the glut of animation being produced by the Eastern Block nations of Europe and the left side of the country formerly known as the USSR. I mean, yeah, the styles have become increasingly fragmented as the countries continue to divide, conquer, and split apart from one another like malignant cancer cells, but on the whole it's still got your basic big eyes, ridiculous boobs and long skinny legs formula at the heart. The Latvians are really going out on a limb and doing pronounced camel toes now, but I really feel you gotta draw the line somewhere. Not that there's anything wrong with being sexy, but at some point the actual anatomy must supersede wanton artistic lust. But as long as there are pubescent teenage boys being produced in this world, you can't go wrong with scantily clad chicks—cheapest marketing tool in the book.

Intention:
In the end, I believe it's having a pronounced effect on sexism in America. I can't say the same for certain countries in South America, but I don't live there, nor do I have any friends who live there, so it's not exactly fair for me to make a blanket statement with worldwide implications. This isn't to say I wouldn't like to live in South America, because I do consider Galapagos to be a fine place indeed, or at least what I've seen of the little Ecuadorian satellite from National Geographic and assorted shows on the Discovery Channel. C'mon, who wouldn't want to frolic in the sun and surf with marine iguanas or go tortoise-tipping in the drunken dead of night? Although, taking into account the physical proportions of a Galapagos tortoise, I think the latter activity must involve one of those Taurine-based energy drinks mixed with vodka.

CITY SERIES

CHOCOLATE SKATEBOARDS

ARTIST: EVAN HECOX

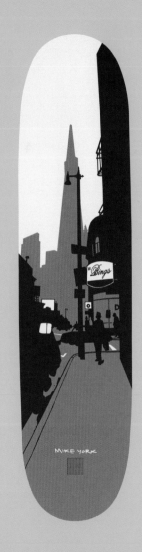

MIKE YORK

KEENAN MILTON

chocolate

RICHARD MULDER

metric
skateboards

Artist: Sandro Grison

Sandro Grison
Metric/Olive

Influences:

My influences come from the relationships and interactions I've acquired through skateboarding. I got my first big chance to design decks in 1995 when I was thirteen years old. I was at a skateboard camp, the first one of its kind in Canada. (Now they're everywhere.) I hooked up with some really nice people who were starting up a deck company and I showed them my sketchbook. At that time, cartoon and character-type graphics were really popular because a lot of younger kids like myself were getting into skateboarding. Now I think more companies are tending to the older, mature crowd and putting out simpler designs with a cleaner look, with the exception of World Industries' Flame Boy and Wet Willy, which the kids go crazy for.

Inspiration:

I get inspired by the freedom of skateboarding—being out with my friends and everyone going off, having a good time. This same sense of freedom is brought out in my artwork. If you look at my art through the years, you can see how I'm exploring something different all the time. I don't think I have a set trademark style yet, although I hope I'll find it soon. Total freedom.

Intention:

I'm working on the unthinkable right now. That is, trying to give recognition to a Canadian skateboard company in this fast-paced industry based on image. It's like there's no such thing as starting at the bottom in this business anymore. For a skate company to last it has to have major financial backing or a huge icon like professional skateboarder Ryan Smith to get kids hyped on it. Right now, I'm doing graphics that will get the name and logos of the smaller companies noticed. Once that's set, I'll have more freedom and do heavier graphic designs, not emphasizing the logo so much. Getting too risky can send a small skateboard company to the ground; I've seen it happen. It's almost like you have to earn the right to be risky. The best examples I can think of are Mark Gonzales' new company Crooked and Marc Johnson's company enjoi; these guys are amazing at skateboarding and have done so much for the sport that they can pretty much put anything on the bottom of a board and kids will be hyped on it. Their companies will last as long as they do.

olive
skateboards

Artist: Sandro Grison

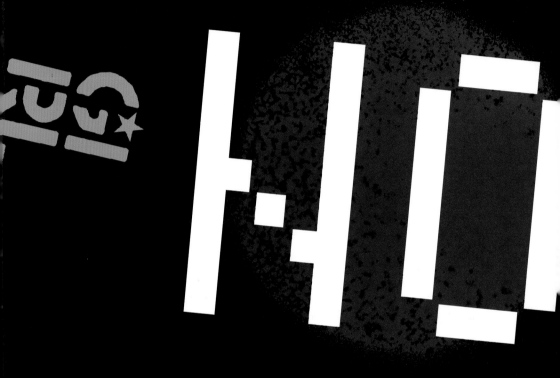

Girl

girl

modern sign series

artist: tony larson

girl

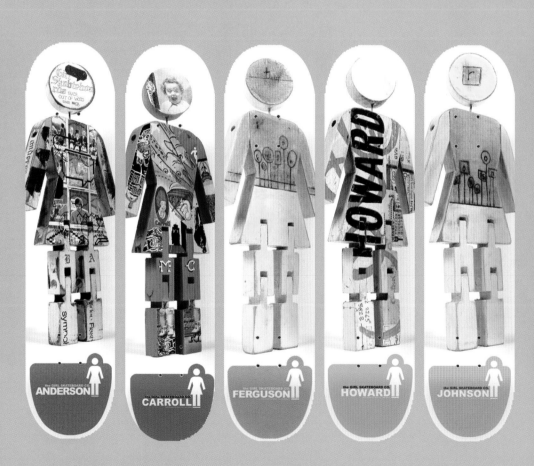

wooden OG series

artists: the girl art dump

girl

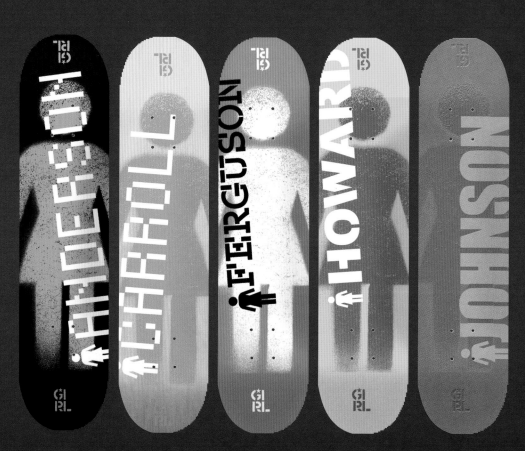

stencil series

artists: andy jenkins & tony larson

enjoi

saint
artist: marc johnson
pro: rodney mullen

sinner
artist: marc johnson
pro: rodney mullen

sinner

Rookie Skateboards
Carny
Artist:Andre Razo

Rookie Skateboards
Socks
Artist: Princess Tina

Rookie Skateboards
Splatch
Artist: Perks

Rookie Skateboards
Space Bunny
Artist: Dalek

media skateboards
RETIREMENT
SERIES
ARTIST: BRIAN JONES

tom krauser
media skateboards retirement plan

adam mcnatt
media skateboards retirement plan

gary smith
media skateboards retirement plan

jake stewart
media skateboards retirement plan

media skateboards
ROCKER SERIES
ARTIST: BRIAN JONES

5BORO

5boro
Hoodies
Artist: Ross Perran

" Deck designs feature an attractive scale and dimension to work with. The 'Empire' and 'Paint-By-Number Taxi' were perfect images for their vertical and horizontal attributes conveying height and speed."
— Zona Design

5boro
Empire
Artist: Zona Design

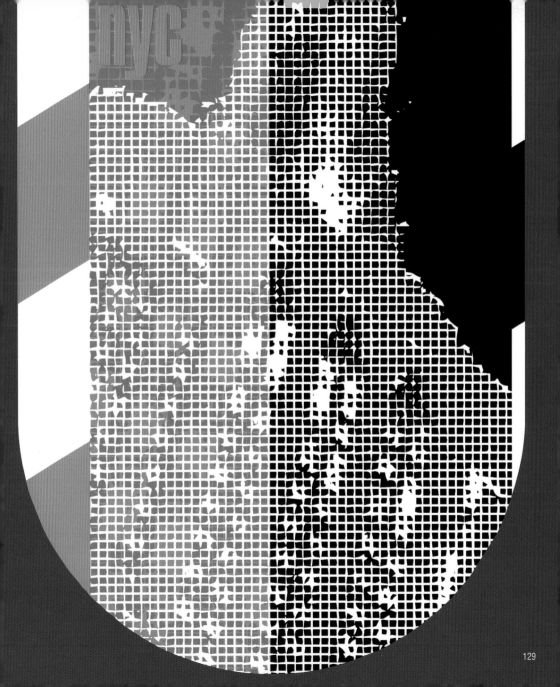

We are influenced by motion and its cause.

5boro
Paint by Numbers
Artist: Zona Design

5boro
5 train
Artist: Karenlee Stern

KARENLEE STERN
ARTIST, 5BORO SKATEBOARDS

Influences:
I have really been interested in and am getting a lot more involved in stenciled graffiti; I like the rawness and complexity of it. If I had to say who has influenced me, shit, I don't know. But I have to say that these guys get me hot: Banksy, Futura, Phil Frost, Chris Yormi... there are so many.

Inspiration:
Deck design is an underappreciated form of artwork. There are amazing artists out there and this form of expression needs more attention. It's great to see those boards out there that aren't mass-produced. It's rad to see kids riding on one–of–a–kind pieces of art.

Intention:
My intentions were to make it look stenciled/silk screened, I wanted it to seem like it was not mass-produced or rather that it was hand done. Plus it was for 5boro and they're a NYC based company so why not a subway. They're everywhere just like skateboarders.

Deathbox   Artist: David Hackett

Ato

FIRECRA

2 IN

0. 28

mic

CKERS

H

Chocolate
Fireworks **Series**
Artist: Evan Hecox

YORK
star
BOMB

Mulder
MARS
ROCKET

Monke Skateboards
Superhero 3D series
Artist: K.C. Chan

Birdhouse

All boards & series
Artists: Sean Cliver & Jeremy Klein

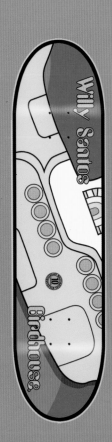

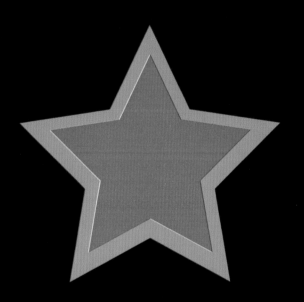

Planet Earth
Artist: Ky Baker

Planet Earth
Artist: Ky Baker

The clock's ticking!
It's your ball! The
computer is on defense.
Find an opening. Shoot!
Score a basket!

AESTHETICS SKATEBOARDS
BARBIER

9-volt-transistor battery, not included.

Aesthetics
Game Series 2
Artist: Alex Aronovich

It's the Big Game!
You're the ball carrier!
Computer's on defense!
Avoid tacklers!
Score a touchdown!

AESTHETICS SKATEBOARDS
IGLETON

9-volt-transistor battery, not included.

AESTHETICS SKATEBOARDS
SINGLETON

Aesthetics
Game Series 2
Artist: Alex Aronovich

Run downfield.
Beat computer-
controlled
defense.
Kick & score!

AESTHETICS SKATEBOARDS

TAYLOR

9-volt-transistor battery, not included.

Aesthetics
Game Series 2
Artist: Alex Aronovich

Computer pitches
curves or fastballs!
Swing away!
Run the bases.
Home Run!

ÆSTHETICS SKATEBOARDS
WELSH

9-volt-transistor battery, not included.

This series was approached in much the same way as
the first series. This time, we were using the old handheld sports videogames from the late
70s/early 80s. This time the decks would have an athletic theme in addition to the nerdiness
of the videogames. As he did with the first videogame series, Sal Barbier picked the best
game for himself... typical.
—Alex Aronovich, Artist

ZOO YORK
FIVE BOROUGH SERIES
ARTIST: ELI M. GESNER

ZOO YORK
FIVE BORO THOROUGHBRED
CROOKLYN / BROOKLYN

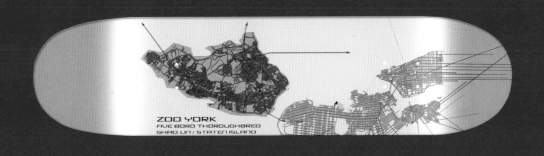

ZOO YORK
FIVE BORO THOROUGHBRED
SHAD LIM / STATEN ISLAND

M·01

PREMIUM

s k a t e b o a r d s

MADE AND OPERATED
BY SKATEBOARDERS
FOR SKATEBOARDERS
SINCE 1996.

Premium Skateboards
Photo Reality Series
Artist: Patrice Dufresne

Premium Skateboards
Cart Series
Artist: Patrice Dufresne

Patrice Dufresne
Art Director: Premium Skateboards

Inspiration:
Nothing in particular. What I usually do is pick a subject, do visual research on it and then try to integrate the elements. It can be a picture, a drawing, sketch, logo, all from various sources. There are different ways to proceed depending on what graphic you want to achieve.

Influences:
Celtic art, tribal art, deconstructive, old magazine iconography, propaganda imagery, alternative music imagery, experimental work of designers, similar to David Carson.

Intention:

Personally, I want to make graphic images that have meaning, things that make people stop to think. I don't want it to simply be eye candy. I want the design to stand on its own but still function as part of the whole company concept. For one of my favorite series, reality show, we wanted to create something controversial to provoke people. The Pierre-Luc Gagnon board was on the obsession of America with guns and weapons. Max Dufour's board was on mass marketing. Alex Gavin's board was on drug abuse and Eric Mercier's board was on youth and violence. The series worked out pretty well. Mercier's board got a lot of attention. With our new high definition screen process printing, it was the first time that photographic collage could be reproduced at such an accurate level.

Skateboard graphic design is a really important aspect of selling boards but it's not the only one. The market is getting bigger everyday. Today, skateboarders start younger and stop older. There are core skateshop and « corporate » shops in the marketplace. You have to try to get the customer's attention and it's a pretty hard job! To stand out, you clearly have to know who your target is and what they're looking for. Amazing graphics sometimes don't find instant success. The product quality also has to stand on its own. The opposite is also true. Some companies don't seem to care about the image they project. Graphically, I think you have to find your own style and stick to it because kids rely on a stable company image. You sometimes have to shut your designer eye and think the way a kid thinks.

Image is not everything. Skateboard graphics are important because they're usually the first and last thing kids will remember. But there's also the product quality, the team riders, the advertising investment, the distribution channels, the community integration, their complementary product line, the guarantee policy, etc.

PÉRONÉ

TIBIA

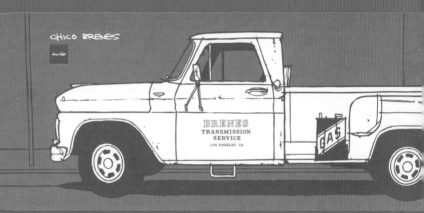

Chocolate
Auto **Series**
Artist: Evan Hecox

Chocolate
Auto **Series**
Artist: Evan Hecox

IMPALA

Chocolate
Auto Series
Artist: Evan Hecox

Keenan Milton

Scott Johnston

Richards Mulder

HABANA

Mike York

girl

Modern Chair series
Artist: Tony Larson

Influences:

I'm lucky enough to be surrounded by the people who I feel are the best designers out there, anywhere. I'm serious about that. I think about what they may say about something I come up with, so they'd have to be my biggest influence. However, I'm inspired by things I see on the freeway everyday.

Inspiration:

I'm a fan of a lot of the elements of '60s design in general, so doing a series with the architecture of that time as the subject was a cinch. I just had so much fun drawing all of those outrageous roadside characters. The same inspiration came into play when I did the *Modern Chair* Series. Fun, fun, fun.

Intention:

As someone who grew up admiring the graphics on skateboards that I rode my whole life, it would be nice to hear that a kid not only liked the quality of his new board but was also into the art too. If a kid was inspired to become an artist because of graphics I did, I'd pretty much cry, I think.

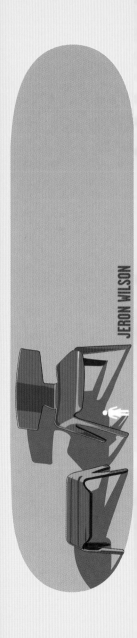

JERON WILSON

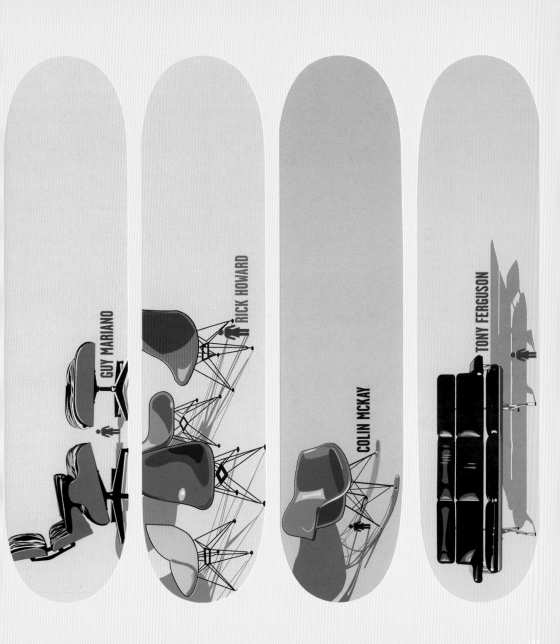

FIGHT SERIES

ROOKIE SKATEBOARDS

ROOKIE NYC

Artist: Elska Sandor

FIGHT SERIES
ROOKIE SKATEBOARDS

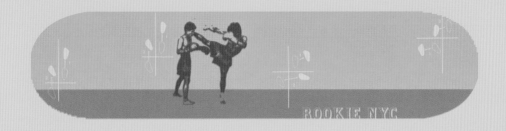

Artist: Elska Sandor

Artist: Beci Orpin

FIGHT SERIES

Artist: Elska Sandor

FIGHT SERIES

Artist: Elska Sandor

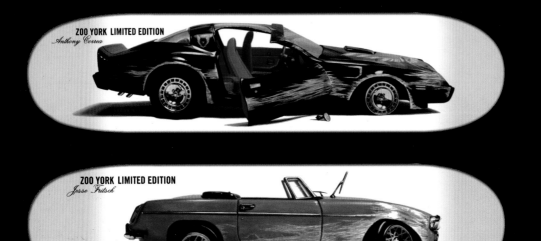

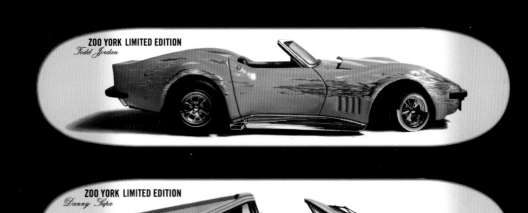

Zoo York   Artist: Eli M. Gesner

THE ZOO YORK INSTITUTE

ZOO YORK

THE ZOO YORK CREW

PANG   BROWN   FRITSCH   CORREA   SUPA   BASSETT   JORDAN

enjoi

minimal
artist: marc johnson
pro: jerry hsu

minimal
artist: marc johr
pro: marc johns

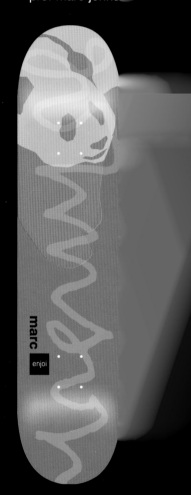

minimal
artist: marc johnson
pro: dave mayhew

minimal
artist: marc johnson
pro: rodney mullen

enjoi

college
artist: marc johnson

leg up!
artist: judson bryan

eyeglasses
artist: judson bryan
pro: jerry hsu

stababox
artist: judson bryan

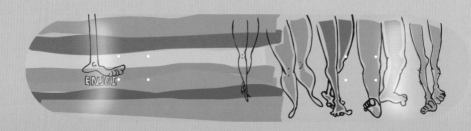

After a while, deck design seems almost futile. The turnaround rate for graphics seems too accelerated, and after all, the art you do for the decks ends up being the very thing that is taken off the board immediately. Designers, for the most part, spend hours and hours sweating over what to put on the bottom of a skateboard, and sometimes a lot of what takes the longest to produce ends up not doing very well sales-wise. It can be disheartening to the designer. I feel the best graphics are the simpler ones. I personally don't care much for intricate illustration. I'm much more a fan of actual graphic design. The composition and the color choices are just as important as the subject matter. To me, simpler is better."

—Marc Johnson, Artist

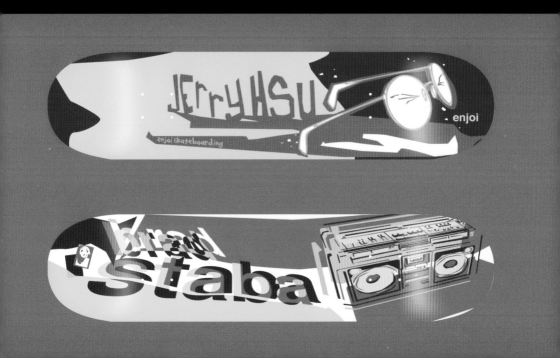

enjoi

toilet
artist: marc johnson
pro: brad staba

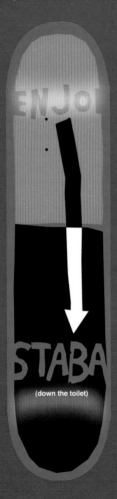

dog
artist: marc johnson
pro: bobby puleo

toilet
artist: marc johnson

bitch'n camaro
artist: marc johns
pro: rodney mulle

Chocolate

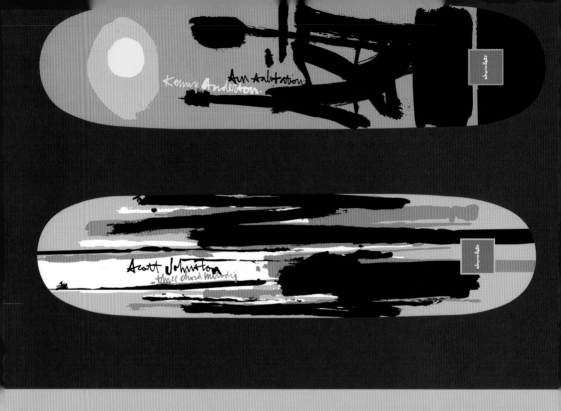

chocolate
artist: evan hecox

Abstract Series

Influences:

I really like design work that has more of a hand-crafted feeling, things that are drawn or painted, hand-lettered type and that sort of thing. I'm influenced by things I see, traveling, taking photos. I like natural forms. Music inspires me too.

Intention:

I see the world in a particular way where I appreciate things that other people might overlook. I'd like for my work to be an expression of how I see things and possibly make other people

see things differently.

I take deck design seriously, as I think the other guys I work with do. I know the board is ultimately a disposable object, but the idea that they are relatively limited in their production life and that they are paint and wood is very attractive to me. I really like doing whole series. It's stressful but the challenge is undeniably addictive. They're little pieces of weird art. I can't wait to see what's next.
— Tony Larson

girl
canada series
artist: tony larson

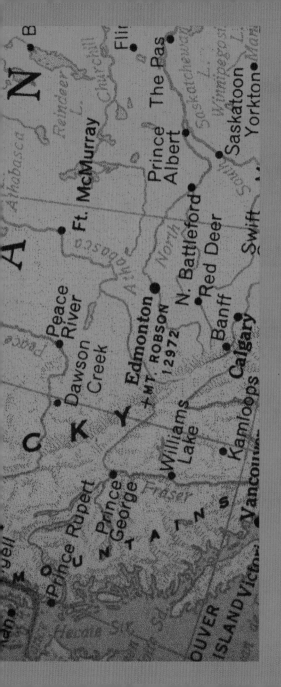

Girl
Fortune Series
Artist: Michael Leon

RICK HOWARD

Series Editor & Creative Direction: Jacob Hoye

Art Editor: Walter Einenkel

Design: Eric Frommelt at Rockpants

Project Managers: Walter Einenkel & Jade Hoye

Rights & Clearances: Michelle Gurney & Elizabeth Vago

Universe Editor: Kathleen Jayes

Many thanks to the following people, without whom, this book could not have come together.

Alex Aronovitch, Ky Baker, Michael Blabac, Charlene Calac, Sean Cliver, Max Dufour, Elska and Catharine, Sandro Grison, David Hackett, John Hampton, Evan Hecox, Brian Jones, K.C., Tony Larson and the Art Dump, Luciano Mor, David Ortiz, Steve Rodriguez, Adam Schatz, and Judy & Sean Tubridy.

Also thanks to:

Ernest Boyd, Hillary Cohen, Geoff Cook, Ralph & Jo Corso, Michelle Dorn, Tim Einenkel, Nick Einenkel, Vanessa Eisman, Wenonah Hoye, Valerie & Richard Hoye, Jeffrey Keyton, Molly Kratofil, Andrew Kuo, George Legrand, Kevin Mangini, Charles Miers, David Moscow, Eva Prinz, Eileen Quast, Michael Rapaport, Adam Rizer, Jeri Rose, Lance Rusoff, Mike & Millie Shivas, Lisa Silfen, Donald Silvey, Pam Sommers, Jean Won, Monica Wong, and Eric Wybenga.

Photo Credits:

Yuri Shibuya: pages 95-96, 181, 182, 220
Michael Blabac: pages 63, 64, 113, 114, 154
Laurel Axen: pages 129, 219
David Boettger: pages 53-54
Bryan Ince: page 32
Aaron Ohrt: page 39
Jay Wescott: page 81
Chris Shonting: page 82
Grandison Tabor: page 102
Patrick O'dell: page 201
Steve Rodriguez: page 202

Correction: MTV Overground Book #1: *MTV Photobooth* was designed by Chie Araki as well as Lance Rusoff & Christopher Truch.